2-12-15
22.00

Ku Gr3

Patterns in the
JUNGLE

by Joyce Markovics

Consultant: Kimberly Brenneman, PhD
National Institute for Early Education Research, Rutgers University
New Brunswick, New Jersey

BEARPORT
PUBLISHING

New York, New York

Credits

Cover, © neelsky/Shutterstock; 3, © thawats/Thinkstock; 4, © Shutterstock; 5, © Artur Cupak/ imagebroker/Corbis; 6, © Michael Langford/Getty Images; 6–7, © Wirepec/Thinkstock; 8–9, © Naypong/Thinkstock; 10–11, © Rod Williams/naturepl.com; 12, © Minden Pictures/ SuperStock; 13, © Morley Read/Alamy; 14–15, © Michael & Patricia Fogden; 16–17, © Anan Kaewkhammul/Shutterstock; 18–19, © Edwin Giesbers/naturepl.com; 20–21, © Thomas Marent/Visuals Unlimited/Corbis; 22–23, © Peter Chew; 24, © Tips Images/Tips Italia Srl a socio unico/Alamy; 25, © Image Quest Marine/Alamy; 26–27, © Joanne Smith/Thinkstock; 28–29, © Dale Morris/Barcroft Media; 30A, © Dirk Ercken/Shutterstock; 30B, © Tim Laman/naturepl. com; 30C, © Dhoxax/Shutterstock; 30D, © Jose Gil/Shutterstock; 31TL, © Wirepec/Thinkstock; 31TR, © ArvydasS/Shutterstock; 31BL, © Morley Read/Alamy; 31BR, © Thomas Marent/Visuals Unlimited/Corbis.

Publisher: Kenn Goin
Senior Editor: Joyce Tavolacci
Creative Director: Spencer Brinker
Design: Debrah Kaiser
Photo Researcher: Michael Win

Library of Congress Cataloging-in-Publication Data

Markovics, Joyce L., author.
  Patterns in the jungle / by Joyce Markovics.
     pages cm. — (Seeing patterns all around)
  Includes bibliographical references and index.
  ISBN-13: 978-1-62724-338-4 (library binding)
  ISBN-10: 1-62724-338-0 (library binding)
  1. Pattern perception—Juvenile literature. 2. Shapes—Juvenile literature. 3. Jungles—Juvenile literature. I. Title.
  BF294.M373 2015
  516.15—dc23

                          2014009094

For more information, write to Bearport Publishing Company, Inc., 45 West 21st Street, Suite 3B, New York, New York 10010. Printed in the United States of America.

10 9 8 7 6 5 4 3 2 1

Contents

Finding Patterns in the Jungle

Patterns can be shapes, colors, or sizes that repeat.

You can see patterns all around the jungle.

4

Frogs in a row make a pattern.

One stripe on a caterpillar is not a pattern.

It does not repeat.

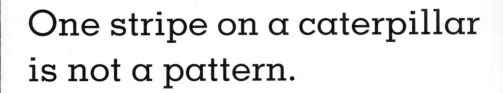

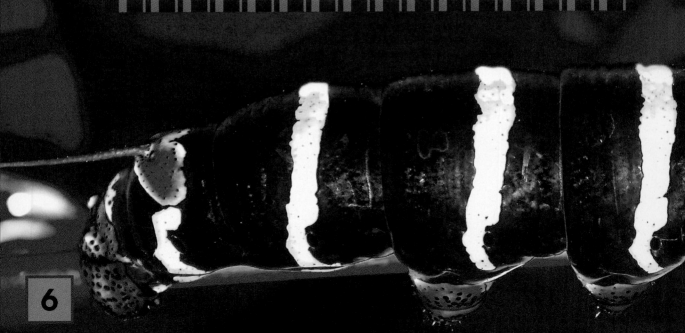

However, many stripes on a caterpillar make a pattern.

Black, white.

The colored stripes repeat.

They make an **alternating** pattern.

8

Parrots resting on
a branch make an
alternating pattern, too.

They face different
directions.

Back, front.

The pattern continues.

A millipede is a long animal with many legs.

When it curls up, its body goes round and round.

It makes a **spiral** pattern.

A colorful bird walks through the jungle.

The blue dots on its tail make a pattern of ovals.

The stripes on a snake's body make a colorful pattern.

Black, yellow, black, red.

14

The pattern repeats over and over.

15

A deer stops by a stream.

It has white spots on its coat.

They are different sizes and shapes.

They make an **irregular pattern**.

Fruit bats flap their wings
to fly through the jungle.

The wings change shape
as they open and close.

18

The different shapes
form a pattern.

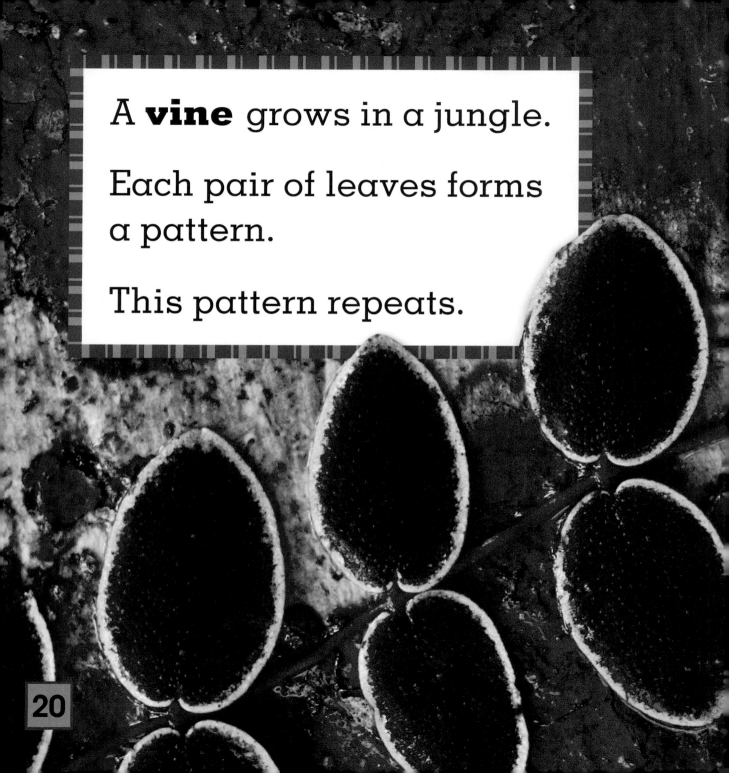

A **vine** grows in a jungle.

Each pair of leaves forms a pattern.

This pattern repeats.

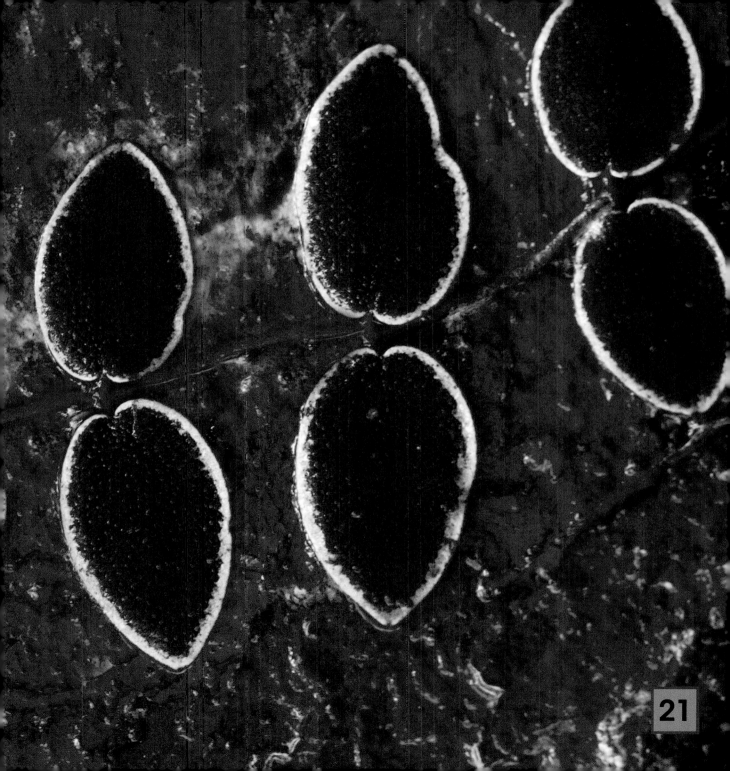

21

Some patterns include different shapes.

An insect's back has a pattern.

22

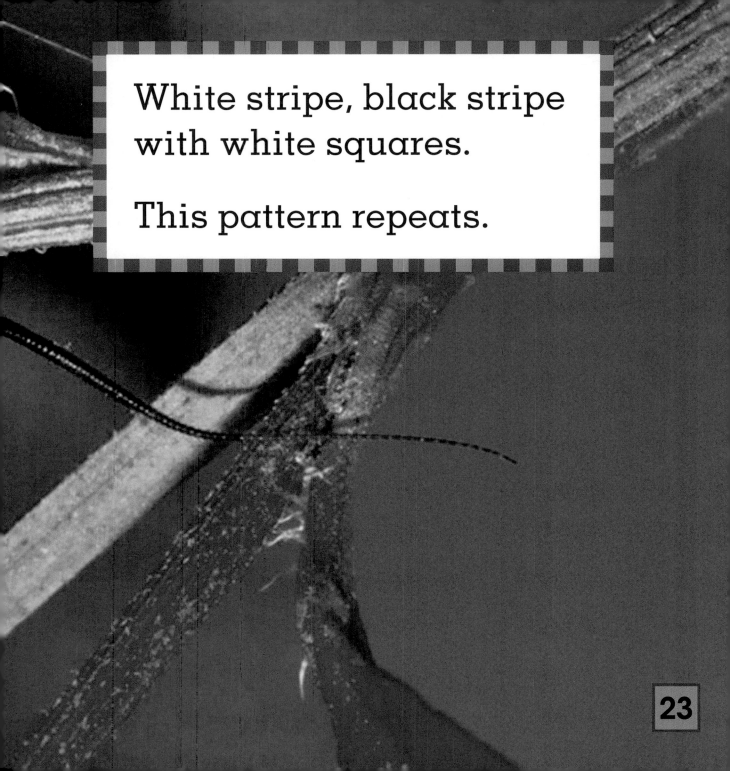

White stripe, black stripe with white squares.

This pattern repeats.

Patterns can be very small.

The rows of scales on a lizard make a tiny pattern.

This pattern goes on and on.

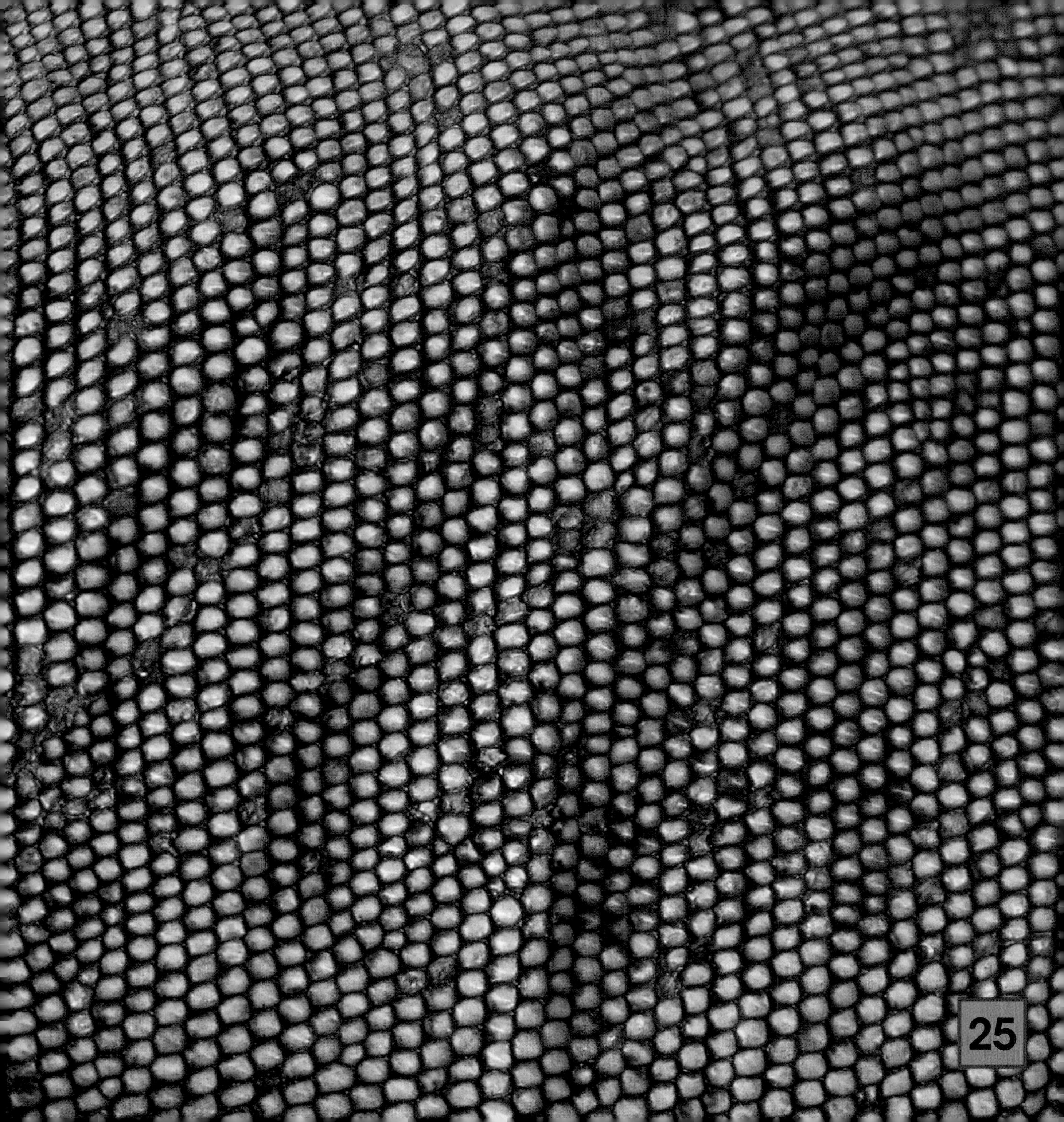

The wings of a butterfly can have different patterns.

What patterns do you see?

Lemurs running through the forest make a pattern.

Up, down.

Patterns are up, down, and everywhere in the jungle!

29

Look at the pictures. Each one shows a kind of pattern that can be found in the jungle. Match each pattern with the correct picture.

1. striped pattern

3. oval pattern

2. spiral pattern

4. irregular pattern

Answers are on page 32.

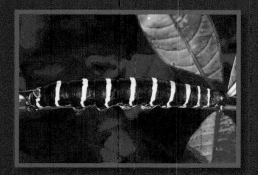

alternating (AWL-tur-*nayt*-ing) changing back and forth, such as between two colors

irregular pattern (ih-REG-yuh-lur PAT-urn) a pattern that has one or more similar parts unequal in size, shape, or in the way they are arranged

spiral (SPYE-ruhl) winding or circling around a center

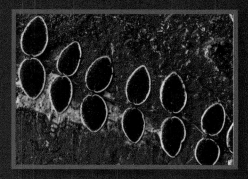

vine (VINE) a plant with a long stem that grows along the ground or by attaching itself to trees

31

Index

Read More

Cleary, Brian P. *A–B–A–B–A: A Book of Pattern Play.* Minneapolis, MN: Millbrook Press (2010).

Harris, Trudy. *Pattern Fish.* Minneapolis, MN: Millbrook Press (2000).

Learn More Online

To learn more about patterns in the jungle, visit
www.bearportpublishing.com/SeeingPatternsAllAround

About the Author

Joyce Markovics and her husband,
Adam, live along the Hudson River
in Tarrytown, New York.

Answers for Page 30:

1. C; 2. B; 3. D; 4. A